A Simple
Rhyming Dictionary

by Sue Palmer and ... Low

How this dictionary works

The letters of the alphabet are at the top of each page. If the letters are coloured red, you will find words beginning with those letters on the page.

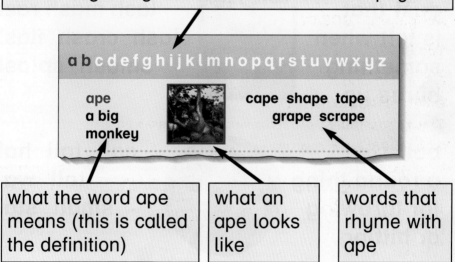

a b c d e f g h i j k l m n o p q r s t u v w x y z

ape
a big
monkey

cape shape tape
grape scrape

| what the word ape means (this is called the definition) | what an ape looks like | words that rhyme with ape |

There is a list of all the rhymes
found in this book on page 24.

LONGMAN

ape
a big
monkey

cape shape tape
grape scrape

ark
Noah's
floating home

bark dark lark
mark park shark
spark

ash
dust that
is left when
something
burns up

bash cash dash
lash mash rash
clash crash flash
smash splash

ball
a round thing
for throwing
or hitting

call fall hall
tall wall
small stall

bee
a buzzing
insect

fee knee see
free three

blade
the sharp
part of
a knife

fade made
shade wade
grade spade
trade

blue
the colour of the sky

cue due
clue glue true

boil
to heat water
until it bubbles

coil foil
oil soil
spoil

cot
a baby's
bed

dot got hot
lot not pot
rot shot tot
blot clot plot
slot spot trot

cow
an animal
that gives
us milk

bow how now
ow! pow! row
sow vow wow!
brow

crust
the outside
of a slice
of bread

bust dust gust
just must rust
trust

cub
a baby lion,
bear or fox

pub rub tub
club scrub
shrub

cuff
the end
of a sleeve

chuff huff puff
bluff fluff gruff
scruff scuff stuff

dog
an animal
that barks

bog fog
hog jog log
clog frog
slog smog

down
towards
the ground

gown town
brown clown crown
drown frown

dress
something
to wear

chess less mess
bless dress press

duck
a water
bird

buck chuck luck
muck suck tuck
cluck pluck struck
stuck truck

ear
what you
hear with

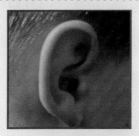

dear fear gear
hear near
tear year
clear spear

eat
what you do
at meal times

beat cheat heat
meat neat seat
wheat
bleat treat

end
finish

bend lend
mend send
blend spend

face
where your
eyes, nose
and mouth are

lace pace
race
grace place
space trace

fan
something
that moves
air about to
keep you cool

ban can man
Nan pan ran tan
than van
bran flan Gran
plan scan

fawn
a baby
deer

dawn lawn
yawn
drawn prawn

fry
to cook in
fat in a
frying pan

by my shy why
cry dry fly
sky sly spy try

gap
a small space

cap lap map
nap rap tap
wrap yap zap!
clap flap scrap
slap snap strap
trap

gate
a type of
door
(outside)

date hate
late mate
crate plate
skate state

grin
a big smile

bin chin din fin
pin shin sin tin
thin win
skin spin twin

ground
the earth
under your
feet

found hound
mound pound
round sound

hand
part of your
body at the
end of
your arm

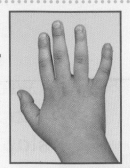

band land
sand
brand gland
grand stand
strand

hide
to move out
of sight

ride side
tide wide
bride glide
pride slide
stride

hook
a place where
you can hang
something

book cook
look rook
shook took
brook crook

hop
to jump
about on
one foot

bop chop cop
mop pop shop
top
clop crop drop
flop plop prop
slop stop

hut
a little
house

but cut gut jut
nut rut shut tut
strut

ice
frozen
water

dice lice mice
nice rice
price slice spice
thrice twice

ill
not well

bill fill gill hill
kill mill pill quill
sill till will
drill frill grill shrill
spill still thrill

ink
comes
out of a pen
so you
can write

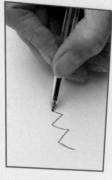

chink link mink
pink rink sink
think wink
blink brink clink
drink shrink slink
stink

jar
a glass
container
for food

bar car far tar
scar spar star

jeep
a car that
can drive
over rough
land

beep deep keep
peep seep
sheep weep
bleep creep sleep
steep sweep

jump
to lift both
feet off the
ground at
once

bump dump hump
lump pump
thump
clump plump
slump stump

kid
a baby
goat

did hid
lid rid
grid skid
slid squid

king
a man who
rules a
country

ping ring sing
thing wing
bring cling fling
sling spring
sting string

kit
a set of
things

bit fit hit
knit lit pit
quit sit wit
grit slit spit
split twit

lime
a small,
sour, green
fruit

chime mime
time
crime grime
slime

lunch
a meal in the
middle of
the day

bunch hunch
munch punch
brunch crunch
scrunch

mole
a little
animal that
digs under
the ground

dole hole
pole role
vole whole
stole

moon
it shines in
the sky
at night

noon soon
croon spoon
swoon

mug
a big cup

bug chug dug
hug jug lug
rug thug tug
drug glug plug
shrug slug
smug snug

name
what
someone
is called

came fame game
lame same
shame tame
blame flame frame

nest
where a
bird lives

best chest pest
rest test vest
west zest
crest

night
when it
is dark –
the opposite
of day

fight knight light
might right sight
tight
bright flight
fright slight

nine
a number

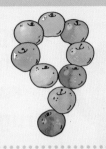

dine fine line
mine nine pine
shine vine wine
spine

oat
a cereal
eaten by
people and animals

boat coat goat
moat
bloat float gloat
stoat throat

old
not young

bold cold fold gold
hold sold told
scold

out
not in

pout shout
clout scout snout
spout sprout
stout trout

paw
an animal's
foot

jaw law raw
saw thaw
claw draw flaw
straw

14

peak
the top of
a mountain

beak leak weak
creak freak
sneak speak squeak
streak

plank
a long
piece of
wood

bank sank tank
thank yank
blank clank drank
prank stank

plum
a small,
sweet,
purple fruit

chum gum hum
mum rum sum
tum yum
drum glum scrum
scum slum strum

quack
the sound
a duck
makes

back lack pack
rack sack shack
tack
black crack smack
snack stack track

15

queen
a woman
who rules
a country

been keen
seen sheen
green screen

rag
a piece of
torn cloth

bag gag hag
lag nag sag
tag wag
brag drag flag
snag stag swag

rain
drops of
water that
fall from
the sky

chain gain main
pain vain
brain drain grain
plain sprain stain
strain train

rake
a garden
tool

bake cake fake
lake make quake
shake take wake
brake drake flake
snake stake

rat
an animal
with a long
tail and
sharp teeth

bat cat chat fat
hat mat pat sat
that vat
brat flat scat
spat splat

red
the colour
of a strawberry

bed fed led shed
bled shred sled

rock
a big stone

cock dock knock
lock mock
shock sock
block clock
flock stock

sad
not happy

bad dad fad had
lad mad pad
glad

seed
what a
plant grows
from

feed need
reed weed
bleed breed
greed tweed

sheet
a large
piece of
cloth that
goes on
a bed

feet meet
fleet greet sleet
street sweet tweet

shirt
something
to wear

dirt
flirt skirt squirt

shore
where the
land meets
the sea

bore core chore
more sore
tore wore
score snore
store swore

snail
a garden
creature
with a shell

fail hail jail mail
nail pail quail rail
sail tail wail
frail trail

snow
frozen
rain

bow know low
row show
blow crow flow glow
grow slow throw

square
a shape
with four
sides

bare care dare fare
hare mare rare share
flare glare scare
spare stare

stamp
you stick
this on a
letter

Copyright the Post Office

camp champ
damp lamp
ramp
clamp cramp
tramp

19

stew
food cooked
in a pot for
a long time

chew dew few
mew new
blew brew crew
drew flew grew
threw

sun
the shining ball
of fire in the sky

bun fun gun
nun run
spun stun

team
a group of
people who
play together

beam seam
cream dream
gleam scream

thorn
a prickle

born corn horn
torn worn
scorn

20

tick
a mark that
shows your
work is right

chick kick lick
pick quick sick
thick wick
brick click flick
prick slick stick
trick

toy
something
children
play with

boy joy
cloy ploy

up
towards
the sky

cup pup sup

vet
an animal
doctor

bet get jet let met
net pet set wet yet
fret

wave
to greet
someone

cave gave pave
rave save shave
brave grave slave

wig
hair that
is not
your own

big dig fig
gig pig
sprig swig twig

x-ray
a picture of
someone's
insides

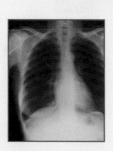

bay day hay
jay lay may pay
ray say way
clay play pray
spray stay stray
sway tray

yam
a sweet
potato

dam ham jam
ram wham!
clam cram pram
scram slam spam
swam tram

yell
a loud
shout

bell fell hell
sell shell tell well
smell spell

zip
this fastens
or does up
clothes

chip dip hip lip
nip pip rip ship
sip tip whip
clip drip flip grip
skip slip trip

zoo
a place
where you
can see
wild animals

boo coo moo
shoo too

23

Index of rhymes

a
-ace 6
-ack 15
-ad 17
-ade 3
-ag 16
-ail 19
-ain 16
-ake 16
-all 2
-am 22
-ame 13
-amp 19
-an 6
-and 8
-ank 15
-ap 7
-ape 2
-ar 10
-are 19
-ark 2
-ash 2
-at 17
-ate 7
-ave 22
-aw 14
-awn 6
-ay 22

e
-eak 15
-eam 20
-ear 5
-eat 5
-ed 17
-ee 2
-eed 18
-een 16
-eep 10
-ell 23
-end 6
-ess 5
-est 13
-et 21
-ew 20

i
-ice 9
-ick 21
-id 11
-ide 8
-ig 22
-ight 13
-ill 9
-ime 12
-in 7
-ine 14
-ing 11
-ink 10
-ip 23
-irt 18
-it 11

o
-oat 14
-ock 17
-og 4
-oil 3
-old 14
-ole 12
-oo 23
-ook 8
-oon 12
-op 9
-ore 18
-orn 20
-ot 3
-ound 8
-out 14
-ow (cow) 3
-ow
  (snow) 19
-own 5
-oy 21

u
-ub 4
-uck 5
-ue 3
-uff 4
-ug 13
-um 15
-ump 11
-un 20
-unch 12
-up 21
-ust 4
-ut 9

y
-y 7